This book belongs to:

____

Made in United States
North Haven, CT
26 December 2022

30212195R00065